To, Auntie Greta,

With all my love,

Rachael
xxxx

Published by Atmosphere Publishing
Willis Vean, Mullion, Cornwall. TR12 7DF
Tel: 01326 240 180
www.atmosphere.co.uk
Printed in Italy by L.E.G.O.

The Tamar Bridges into Cornwall

Boat trips. Looe

4

Polverro

Polverro

Polruan

Fowey

Looe fishing boats at dawn

Charlestown

Mevagissey

Mevagissey

Mevagissey

St Iust in Roseland

St Mawes Harbour

Falmouth Docks

Helford

Coverack Harbour

Cadgwith

The Old Lizard Lifeboat House.

Kynance

The Lizard Point

Mullion Storm

Mullion Harbour

St. Michael's Mount

Newlyn

31

Mousehole

Mousehole

Penberth

Lamorna

Land's End   *Long Rock*

Cape Cornwall

Pendour Cove, Zennor

St. Ives

St. Ives

Porthminster Beach

Godrevy

Perranporth

Holywell Beach

Fistral Beach

Newquay Harbour

Newquay

Mawgan Porth

Bedruthan Steps

Constantine Bay

Trevose Lighthouse

Padstow

Daymer Bay

Rock

Port Isaac

Tintagel Head

Boscastle

Millook

Bude

Widemouth Bay